poems

lures

Adam Vines

Louisiana State University Press

Baton Rouge

Published by Louisiana State University Press
lsupress.org

LSU Press Paperback Original

DESIGNER: Mandy McDonald Scallan
TYPEFACE: Calluna

Cover image by John Sekutowski/Unsplash

The author is grateful to the editors of the following publications, in which the poems listed first appeared: *32 Poems:* "Prayer for the New Acolyte"; *100 Natures Mortes in Verse:* "Remains"; *Action, Spectacle:* "My Father's Trowel," "Coursing the Joints," "The Silent Stones," and "Memory Care"; *Atlanta Review:* "After Losing a Child"; *Cellpoems:* "Worm on the Hook"; *Double Dactyl:* "Blinky"; *Ecotone:* "Question from a Bowl of Beans"; *Five Points:* "My Father's Rod: Fishing the Skinny Moon"; *Freshwater Review:* "Crab Stakes"; *Iron Horse Review:* "The Silents"; *Kenyon Review:* "River Elegy"; *Madcap Review:* "Tea Party"; *Mead:* "The Golden Years"; *Measure:* "The Drought"; *North American Review:* "Apprenticeship"; Norwegian Writers' Climate Campaign: "Invasives"; *Pleiades:* "Preservation for the Heartbroken"; *Poetry:* "Lures" and "River Politics"; *Smartish Pace:* "Sabbatical Poem [or] Time, You Mosaic of Clicking Ignitions and Broken Shoelaces"; *Southern Humanities Review:* "This Little Piggy"; *Southern Review:* "Last Day at Brinkwood"; *Southwest Review:* "Anti-Aubade"; *Sou'wester:* "'Infant Son, Born and Died May 3, 1872'"; *storySouth:* "Maintenance for the Heartbroken," "Our Boat," and "Tithing Beers"; *Terminus:* "No Wake Zone" and "The Hipster Pragmatist and the Emo Poet Blunt Their Teeth after Three Bottles of Mad Dog 20/20 and Adequate Sex"; *Town Creek Review:* "Pigeons at Fat Sam's"; *Unsplendid:* "To the Scholar Who Explains His Poem to Me before He Writes It"; *Waccamaw:* "Tell Me a Story"; *Who Will Speak for America:* "Morning Question in Bed after the Women's Marches across America."

The following poems have been reprinted in anthologies: "Anti-Aubade," "Golden Years," and "River Politics," in *Language Lessons;* "This Little Piggy," in *Verse Daily;* "River Politics," in *Vinegar and Char: Southern Food in Verse.*

Library of Congress Cataloging-in-Publication Data
Names: Vines, Adam, author.
Title: Lures : poems / Adam Vines.
Description: Baton Rouge : Louisiana State University Press, [2022]
Identifiers: LCCN 2021022471 (print) | LCCN 2021022472 (ebook) | ISBN 978-0-8071-7689-4 (paperback) | ISBN 978-0-8071-7725-9 (pdf) | ISBN 978-0-8071-7726-6 (epub)
Subjects: LCGFT: Poetry.
Classification: LCC PS3622.I55 L87 2022 (print) | LCC PS3622.I55 (ebook) | DDC 811/.6—dc23
LC record available at https://lccn.loc.gov/2021022471
LC ebook record available at https://lccn.loc.gov/2021022472

lures

contents

lures

Maintenance for the Heartbroken

Consider the houses we put together,
the maintenance we do and don't do,
the rotten eaves replaced, the shutters
that a friend half-scraped three years ago
before the night took him back
to needling that vein he thought he'd closed.
Consider the toilets we spray with blue
then flush down, the ball of our love's hair
we snake up from the shower drain
and lift in a pinch of nape
as if it were a mouse. Consider what we see now
at 2:00 a.m. in the kitchen, the grout
we might or might not finally clean; the bond
that holds this floor together will remain,
soiled or not, we know. Consider the neighbor's generator
still chugging after they have long gone to bed,
though the power to our houses is back on.
Consider the meat and milk that didn't go bad.
We will hear the engine sputter and cease before dawn.
Consider the storm that dumped nine inches
of snow in Lubbock, Texas, today, yes, Texas.
Consider the woman in Montana tonight
curled into the hollow spoon of her husband
after telling him of her affair.
Consider her lover as merely a context
for another repair. Consider finding ourselves
not as agency but as a slow cracking of our shells
from the weather of our lives.
Consider a sand dune that takes its shape
when the clouds drift, allowing the moon
to untuck its light. Consider how the clouds
seem to occupy the same space
as that moon, despite their distance,
how we distinguish liquids, solids, gases

by their properties, their distances apart,
the way they veil and unveil themselves to us,
though, at times, like tonight, we find
in our chests that they must be compliant
to their elemental change
but at their core are just the same.

My Father's Rod: Fishing the Skinny Moon

—in memory of Vann Allen Vines

While waiting on the Opelousa bite,
or channel cats would do, our fingertips
plucking our fishing lines below the first
eyes, twitching livers we had hooked and cast
into the river's craw, my father would
relax, the only time I witnessed this.
He'd stretch his legs and dig his heels
and match a Lucky Strike to life. He'd drag
and exhale that the night had pocketed
the moon; the cats would bite. We'd be all right.
I'd dig in deep like him and hum a hymn
I still don't know the name of—nor did he,
I don't believe—but in that dark, that settling
loam and that Alabama clay, that hymn
was ours, and God was there, or not. It didn't matter.
The bills were paid. He held his rod. He'd be all right.

Tell Me a Story

Father, tell me about the Moor
who moored his boat in a moor,
how he ate petrified alligator toes
and hid his prayers in snail shells,
how he turned into a bear, refused to hunt,
spent his days licking the shadows
of crows that stretched before him.

Brother, tell me the one about the woman who planted
her husband's pool cue in the ocher loam
of her childhood creek, the smooth ash knotting
into dogwood, the blue tip's sobering blooms.
Tell me about the woman at the dump,
her eyes large and dark as a mule's,
how she enters our dreams when she gathers our junk.

Mother, tell me about the bricklayer who was taken away
to rebuild the city of God, how he didn't need
a plumb line to lay the golden courses,
how his trowel turned into a crappie when he was done.
But this time let me finish: his son mixed
what he'd learned in Sunday school and comic books
to try to make sense of it all,

wished he were Thor, winged crown of tinfoil on his head,
his father's brick hammer dangling from a belt loop,
how he descended into the underworld
of the basement to find his father
after the burning bush was just burning brush
and the rainbow bridge was merely
the long frown of the morning storm.

My Father's Trowel

It was a magic wand, baton, from which
Retaining walls and symphonies appeared—
But only in his hand, the one I feared—
Prosthesis shearing clangs and twangs, the pitch
Of labor. With the "fucks," the flicks of mud
I mixed too thin, the tamps of bricks and rasps
Of joints, the courses rose, despite my lapses
Back to a time before when the word was "crud"

And cuss words he would hide from me were kept
In stow behind closed doors with Mom. He wore
A tie back then and ran his routes, collecting
Premiums, "beneficiary" the word he swore.
But I can't see that man, that truth, except
Right now, his trowel in my hand, its anger tolling.

River Elegy

—in memory of Jake Adam York

Yesterday, snow,
not stars, fell on Alabama,
but on my slow jam home

over Red Mountain behind a streak
of bread-and-milk-stocked cars
chocked by a "field of white,"

I can't keep from humming
the tune over and over,
replacing *stars* with *snow.*

Tomorrow, I would have driven past
Tuxedo Junction where Erskine Hawkins
might have brassed those *stars*
seventy-five years ago in Ensley

and over viaducts beneath which
hoggers haven't hung rails with black snakes
or pig-iron cars in decades and foundry molds
haven't flushed orange for just as long—

and *on* to the sticks, through hollers
where my kin ripped seams of coal
and piled spoils in rippling rows,
heeling pulp pines in their stead—

and *on* to Beat 10 of the Warrior River
where fish camps outnumber churches,
where a man stepping on another man's land
might see a lightning still hunkered into a bank
or just how deep that river channel is—

and *on* to the dirt road's end
where my kin crawled out of the river,
where I would have cut and split
a seasoned white oak for your visit
and piled rocks for a pit closer to the slough,

so when we would have run
and re-livered that trotline by the skinny moon,
we'd have fire close when we skulled
back to the bank. Then over a skillet
of skeeting yellow cat fillets,

I would have mentioned the rendition
still stuck in my head even today—
Fitzgerald and Armstrong's—
and the absurd snow, and you would have gone on
about *you,* an Alabama privet switch,
driving through Colorado on winter days.

And I bet I would have learned from you
on that night that will never be
what I had to learn on my own today,
that Holiday and Coltrane flirted through
that number, too, and the song owes its breath
to the 1833 Leonids meteor shower,

"the night the stars fell." And I imagine
you would have said what I am thinking now:
that a shower of '33 happens only once
every couple of lifetimes,
and even then it won't happen
if you ain't paying attention.

Prayer for the New Acolyte

—for Mary

Settle my daughter's feet and clenching toes
before the organ's prelude. Lead her doe's
gait—soft, measured—as if on leaves instead
of stone. Lighten her cotta, the sleeves unfed
like open mouths, her hands dry tongues, and tame
her arms outstretched with wonder and the flame.
Give her the grace to light the wick then walk
away and sit through creeds, the silent stalk
of prayers, the sermon's knife and recompense.
And in the preacher's final words, our stench
of sins the benediction threatens to relieve,
bestow her strength to snuff the flame and still believe.

Lures

—in memory of Scott Harris

Last summer's fishing failures dangled from trees:
a Rapala and Jitterbug a stand
of privet paid for, half-ounce jigs with rubber skirts
and jelly worms with wide-gap hooks on ten-pound test
we tithed with overzealous casts at bass.
Then off we'd go (our stringers bare) to find
a yard to cut, a truck to wash, so we could fill
the tackle box we shared again. Today
is 12/12/12, the Mayan end, and I,
a country boy in Brooklyn for the week,
will hail a cab for the first time and think
of cows unnerved by fish we missed
and shouts of "shit" that followed, and dawns to dusks
and always back with you, my childhood friend.
Our girls will never know that pond's deep hole
a baseball diamond now fills—the city leaders' bright
idea—or how their fathers sitting in the bleachers
on Saturdays a couple decades later
can almost feel the stinging nettle against
their thighs, the lunker largemouth sweeping the bed
with her tail while plastic lizards jerk and drag
across the third base line, or how when we
untrain our ears to baseballs cracking bats
and bitchy parents, called strikes and alike,
we hear the peepers sounding off in oaks
on down the way, our mothers' and fathers' voices
calling us home not too far behind or ahead.

After Losing a Child

The sun is winking early daffodils,
the yellow bells the same. The late spring frost
will knock them back, but you are lost
in turning soil, tomato seeds the pills

you plant, your body hunched in shame or prayer.
We haven't talked today. The curtains wrap around
my cheeks like a wimple I can almost bear,
and I am counting prey in webs, the mound

that must have been a moth, the lightning bug,
dirt dauber (its organ pipes upon the eaves)
now all encased, escaping entropy,
the fodder for a coming brood. I dug

into your drawer last week—I must confess—
though you can't hear, and found the ace of spades,
the bookmark I gave you, not black enough these days,
my number scrawled across the back. The window's less

a way to see you now. It's just a wall
like any wall, its molecules intact.
You place a cage around the row you made and ball
your gloves. The garden will beget

what we cannot, despite the cold and rainless days ahead,
and we will sow into ourselves, unsure of how we're fed.

Squatter

In a squatter's heap of trash, I looked for grubs
to fish for bream on beds. Vienna cans
and ripple bottles tossed aside, I dug
through compost only offal and coffee grounds
could make. That sweet death twang pricked up,
the kind of stink you find unspooled across
the logging roads when bucks in rut, thick necks
erect, their senses dulled from estrus in the wind,
would turn their heads and freeze in the headlights' eyes.
I found a nightcrawler, then deeper down,
an open mouth of a minnow trap. I pulled
it free, the belly crushed, a rat snake coiled
inside. Licking the air in frantic swaths,
its tongue, a Bible's ribbon, tasted me.
The snake had shed a skin, the brittle length
half-curled like a mate, a pallid dream.
A couple mouse skulls rattled when I shook
the trap, and tiny vertebrae fell through.
The mice had made the same mistake before
the snake, the opening a vortex. What lured
them to that place, the hole becoming smaller
and smaller until the chicken wire raked across
their backs and they slipped through? And what
would cause the squatter to ditch the minnow trap
(he could have pulled it round again), and what
became of him, the man who squatted on
this square of land when seams of coal went thin?

I want to lie and tell you that I clipped
the wire and let that critter out and watched
it wind away—Rainbow, Rainbow, Rainbow. . . .
But at the time I was a boy with fish
and nothing else much on my mind.

I tossed the trap off to the side without
a care for that rat snake. I found some grubs
and caught some fish.
                        I know now what it's like
to crawl into a hole and hope it will
open to something new, but never does
and narrows, scraping up your back. I've seen
the belly crushed. I've curled up in a ball,
while staring at what someone shed for me,
a pallid dream of you who loved me once, the me
who wouldn't cut the wire, the you I left inside.

Sunday

Squirrels rattle the feeder.
The peace plant curls
into itself. Tomorrow's shirt
needs pressing. The fish from last night

lingers in the sink, the wine uncorked,
going stale. You'll come home from church
and shopping and ask what I did today.
I'll say, "nothing" and, for once, mean it.

To the Scholar Who Explains His Poem to
Me before He Writes It

But words came halting forth, wanting Invention's stay,
Invention, Nature's child, fled step-dame Study's blows,
And others' feet still seemed but strangers in my way.
—Sir Philip Sidney

He wants to underlay Orestes in the poem.
Epistle—yeah, he says, to the son he tries to sway
to hate his mother. Alexandrines, anacoluthon,
slippery substitutions with anapests, trochees,
alveolar—spirants, shit!—sibilants, feminine endings
(an extra foot for emphasis, one fourteener couplet),
he'll pull out all his tricks. The form? a blank-verse sonnet
of sorts. The turn will be a delving into modern,
devalued love, his story: why he left his lover and the boy.
The boy must really miss his stand-in father, friend
for years. Describing fights (the truth!) in Dublin streets,
the mother's spells, her lack of meds, dissolving all
the questions. . . . "*How* will you persuade the reader to *feel,*"
I wedge, "you'll need more lines. Your lover has another—
right?—in her bed, a stand-in just like you. Perhaps
the boy would love to kill you all." "*Feel?*" he asks.
"The form—the twists and turns—suffices in my absence!"

The Drought

The hostas lip their purple sex despite
their curling leaves, today more brown than green,
and trillium are gone, their shriveled stems tar-black.
Even the poison oak falls limp from trunks.
The sugar maples drop their yellow skirts
on the yellow lawn, and the yellow lab across
the street unhinges his spine, dirt-angels nose
to ass and back again, again, again,
the rising dust his futile pleasure's ghost.
And inside, you wait for me: your temp. is right,
the sheets pulled back, my pillow fluffed, while low
Sinatra croons "A Garden in the Rain."

This Little Piggy

—for Mary

Like a cat lured by its tail,
my daughter doesn't yet know
her feet are hers. She chews
and slobbers on these strange orphans,
slaps them together
as a punished student would
chalkboard erasers.

In her crib, hands clasp feet
in a spire of unstable flesh,
then she plops to one side,
looks at me then doesn't
through the bars as I kneel,
and I see clearly that the red
in my beard is the red in her curls

but also that *my* daughter
is not *mine,* that love is not possession
or a mere pronoun or an apostrophe
in the sympathetic system of language,
that one day she will realize that her feet
conform to *her* will, *her* heart,
and she will walk away from me.

Tea Party

—for Mary

My daughter is sick again,
but she still asks for tea times:
her great-aunt's cups, the empty tin.
My daughter is sick again.
She says, "I need to choke again."
I hold her hair like flower stems.
My daughter is sick again,
but she still asks for tea times.

Question from a Bowl of Beans

—for Mary

A bite of beans, a long milk draw, and then
a side glance: "What's it like to be a boy?"
she asked. Tiresias first came to mind,
the mating snakes he struck, the female dead,
his seven years in women's flesh that followed.
Didacticism at its worst, I thought,
especially how to explain his lie
to Hera, pleasures of the wee and woo,
and homosocial bonds, the kind
of myth an eight-year-old like mine would dig
then dig at me until I broke, explaining different parts
and dumbass boys, the birds and bees. My wife
was teaching dance that night and would have struck
me blind if I had gone that way. Instead,
I merely said, "it ain't that bad," a lie
of course, then took another bite of beans.
"The penis seems to be a lot of trouble,"
she said while looking down into her bowl.
And, once again, I thought, *deflect.* I could
bring Nana into play and how at eight
I told my class about my front-tail, unzipped
my pants to show them when they said I lied,
Miss Walker's scream, the long walk down the hall,
how Nana let me think I had a tail for years,
until that day when I walked home and Daddy
told me about the penis, the stiff-tailed ways.
I knew "it ain't that bad" would hardly do for this.
I said, "you're right—it is a lot of trouble. Stay away."

Second-Grade Christmas Pageant,
Birmingham, Alabama, 1976

—in memory of Jessica Hayden

When she came strolling in, her hair sprung free,
dashiki waving like a pagan flag
at parents' gasps and "Mammy Ass" from Jimmy's dad,
we all—her donkeys, Mary, wise men, sheep—
fell to our knees and crawled to see what she
had promised us. Her platform heels were clear
with live fish within each. We almost peed
our pants and squealed. We couldn't see the fear

our mothers felt, this surrogate, "a black"
at that, who hugged us all before we hit
the stage, this water-walking woman god
with goldfish hip-sways in her soles. The feed sack
Mama had cut into a tunic bit
my flesh like gnats, and Daddy's belt, a nod

to him, my model, Mama made me wear,
I dared to loosen during curtain call
as a grunt I knew too well exhaled from a dark place
beyond my sight, when I begged our god to the stage.

Blinky

"Grouseleachy," "housebeachy,"
Frederick Biletnikoff
Heard in the huddle from
Snake with his drawl,

One-handed snag, *a, a*
Parthenogenesis,
Mullet on fire, his
Mustache an awl.

Morning Question in Bed after the
Women's Marches across America

—for Mary

"Do we deserve to live?" you ask,
not do we live or how we live,
those I have stumbled through before,
dawn reticulating light through blinds
across the beds I built for your dolls.
Before I trip into an answer,
some softened Hume or backwoods Job,
or try to squeeze from you the doubt,
you blurt out Pilate's wife, the dream
she had, what you recall from Sunday's
service. You say that you woke up
last night from dreams of women dressed
in white all standing in the streets,
and as the light reveals your face,
a bar across your mouth and one
across your eyes, your words dissolve,
reform into a wrinkled sheet

of light I lift above my head to hear
and see beneath three million chant
in unison "our bodies are not yours."
You ask, "What is our only comfort in?"
I can't respond. I hide my face. "In us,"
you say for me with fortitude and grace.

Euphoria of Belief

—after Bosch's *The Conjurer*

His thorny nose points to the pearl he rolls
between his thumb and index finger.
His table's set—the cups, the wand, the frog
as awestruck as the dupe, his mouth

gaping, his back bent back like Bosch's fish
who lounge on land in gluttony.
An owl peers from a wicker basket's hole
and stares at me from centuries back,

its face anemic like a sundried heart,
a patch of whey, and if I squint,
a lazy eight for eyes, infinity.
Most other folks are mesmerized,

some with the pearl, the monkey's studded strap,
its ear-holed hat, but one knows well
the conjurer and snakes his hand across
a Lady's chest and to the jewels

that hang between her breasts. Another man,
dressed like a monk, his scapular
missing a cowl, seems taken with the fist
of God, his eyes locked upward to

the deadened sky, his fingers pinched around
the faux mark's purse. Who are the conies
and who the grifters in this scene and who
lacks faith and who believes that frogs

can leap from tongues? I bend into the scene
as Bosch would hope we'd do. I squint
again, and a boy below the fray, holding
a scopperel, a whirligig,

as if he were an acolyte with a bell snuffer,
becomes a dwarf, a cutpurse who
moved in too late. What seems a paradox—
a man-fish wishing to be seen

as a woman with a key, a monkey-dog,
a monkish thief—is simply what
we are, a conjuring, with sin but just
a con that tricks us to believe.

Anti-Aubade

A crow gouges the lead sky
now smeared pewter and tungsten

with new rips and drags of aluminum
every passing second,

all alloy and amalgam and fusion,
then spit-shined—your shine,

my spit—the crow's eye and caw
cut back to us after it lights on that limb

broken free at the elbow, nubbed
like a gray-veined bust,

how nature might suppose
Balzac caught in his fury

if nature could suppose
or how I now knot Rodin's Balzac

folding into himself with inspiration
with the dead white oak's

overlapping bark, its chippings
and leavings, a slow shed, spread legs,

thick arms, necks, our branchings,
knuckles, cusps and curls and braids,

our inward foldings, our eyes cut away
from one another because they must,

our clothes shed on the shore.
Years from today, this white oak trunk

will fill with worms and woodpeckers,
maybe with this owl whom we hear

in the distance, the one I am flirting with
as my father's father taught me,

(you have heard this before)
or its progeny or progeny's progeny

in a stolen hole, its head unwound.
And with the mourning doves'

swollen breasts and whinnying
on wires we cannot see

but know are there, we devolve—
because, again, we must—from human

to amphibian, our desires now simplified
to the dead-still water in which we submerge

to our noses, to the great rock beneath us
we shimmy and scuttle along, hands

and feet indistinguishable, until ours
meet by chance, and we move closer.

Coursing the Joints

While setting trots and drops for channel cats
on the river where my family spawned, I sculled
the bank, around the bend and past the camps
where city folks launched boats with colors culled
from candy stores and tourist traps, "The Lulled,"
my gramps would say in his last years when wakes
from outboards nearly swamped his jon and bulled
him to the bank. I pulled into the slough
where he would mash his shine and take a nip or ten and lose

himself in jars. The cabin that he built
five decades back from rock he'd hauled and sand
he'd scrapped from roads, the mortar pink from clay,
was torched. Some hunters I ran off the month before
were running dogs for deer and said, "the land
ain't yours." I walked them to the boundary line,
a pistol at their backs. "We'll get you, pussy boy,"
they said. Some empty Bud cans had been tossed
beside a white oak where we nailed and skinned our cats.

The cabin was now just a shell, a porch
of river rocks, a couple walls of shale,
the chimney still intact. Inside, a scorched
bed frame, a deformed stove and fridge. The rails
that held a whittled pistol grip to our hailed
.410—named "Gar Be Gone"—lay on the hearth
beside the lock and barrel. The rest was veiled
with ash and char, but I could see the mortar lips
the inside walls once concealed, where he had jooged with fingertips

and squished the mud between the upturned rocks
where trowels just couldn't fit or when he tipped
the shine while mixing mud and laying rock.
I pressed my knuckles into his, my thumb,
my palm, and bent a brick tie back and forth
until it snapped. I ran my hands across the joints,
from course to course, my fingers spreading out
and snaking through his hands: the fossils he
had left behind, the gift the fire gave back to me.

Last Day at Brinkwood

To become aware of the possibility of the search is to be onto something.
—Walker Percy

A peony busts through the mulch, its leaves
drooping and purple veined, the stem the same.
Hard freeze tonight—the bud won't burst its frame
this year, unclench the red and white it weaves,
this one the first this spring to periscope.
What spiked this bulb and coaxed it through the soil
like the Second Coming, the uncoiling
of arms, the end of days when we will lope

for one last time on Earth and bathe in fire
and burn in lakes? Lost Cove is spuming with desire
below: the frothy streams, the squirrels in rut,
a yelping hen, a tom's vibrato, saltatory strut.
This early bulb will wait another year
to let loose what it sucks back in tonight: the coming on we fear.

The Hipster Pragmatist and the Emo Poet Blunt Their Teeth
after Three Bottles of Mad Dog 20/20 and Adequate Sex

Leaves are more than just leaves—
arbitrary as the arbitrary
letters that invoke them, the letters
suspended, arranged, and, again, suspended
like quivering arrows until bent for meaning like
infinite sets collecting and scattering the infinite.

Leaves are just that: leaves—
matted in a gutter, not matted
by the gutter and christened conceptual found-art, a goodbye
some lame artist names *The Parts of Its Sum,*
not an island colonially clear-cut, not
a snake eating its tail, not one anchored "A"
damming the watershed of animus, not some eternal damning.

Crosses are just that: crosses—
electric chairs painted white; electric
white like Good Friday is only white
while the walls of the church, the white wile
congregating in pews loses interest in the sermon. Congregating
crows beyond the crazed glass catch their eyes. "Eat a murder of crows,"
they think, then ask, "who are these 'brothers and sisters' of mine, I, we, they?"

We are more than just that: we—
two quarks, dualities of light, we, one, two,
blue haze before we burn blue.

Blind

Behind the blind of elaeagnus hedge
marking the line between me and my neighbor,
teens kiss their skinny cigarettes and chew
caps from their beers with molars white as toilets.

The Silents

Her platinum finger-waves fallen, her roots dark as liver,
bearing witness like Nora's I.O.U.
in *A Doll's House,* looking now like a faded star's comb-over,
Anita Page trades Clara Bow her mackerel-blue

brooch for three cigarettes. Thunder
cracks over the delta. Alice Joyce armors
her cheeks with her hands and squats under
a bush, her eyes empty as an itinerant farmer's.

Vamps, virgins, and flappers wait for the curtains
to meet, for the subconscious noises
from critics cueing the Wurlitzer
for the upturned faces of those relegated to vaudeville haze.

The yellowing Friday *Photoplays* burn,
the women's *I do*s and *I can't*s engraved
in their expressions on the covers—words
their lost, soft tongues never had to crave.

Buster Keaton rows up to the shore,
then suddenly—arm raised, hat cocked—
his peevish "Ladies . . . " diffracts the sun-glare
from the firmament painted across the backdrop.

"Infant Son, Born and Died May 3, 1872"

Mowing the grass on Decoration Day,
I passed a row of tiny, speckled headstones.
Beneath one lay the seventh infant son
of T. W. and Kissar Bailey, swaddled
with honeysuckle, browning gardenias,
the gabardine his mother cut and patched
with little sweaters (blue and pink) she'd knitted
over the years, his coffin hewn from clapboards.
I heard the preacher's eulogy, the words'
struggle to ring, the whisper from uncle to aunt.
Passing again, I saw stone lambs asleep
in mounds of ants, their shoulders bent
against the marble's grain. The cutter must
have kept the onionskin tracing and clay *maquette*
after the first few headstones. His pitching tool
in hand, his hammer poised above his head,
he must have thought of imperfections struck in stones.

Invasives

—Bransfield Strait, Antarctica

We know you are below us
concentrating krill: teal
feeding-bubbles twitching
to the surface, perforating chads
in the Antarctic Ocean's
untidy sheet. Do you mistake
the dark ovals of our Zodiaks above you,
the outboards' hummings, and the props'
disturbances for glaciers calving
or a waddle of gentoos porpoising
like pistons in the ocean's machinations?

And how absurd we must look
to your huge eye now upon us
when you breech, our camera lenses
protruding like curious snouts,
our torsos small-bore targets—
maroon parkas ringed with orange life vests—
our stoplight-red research shack
just within your sight, the way it skins
the peninsula's receding knee of ice.

Apprenticeship

He butters up the corners, base
and fishtails, tamps the brick in place,
then rasps the trowel across the joint.
He butters up the corners, base
then slides the chock and plumb line up.
"Boy, scrape my mudboard, keep it wet."
He butters up the corners, base
and fishtails, tamps the brick in place.

At the Customer's Request

Nitrogen-juiced, a specious green,
the zoysia lay there plush and thatched.

Years of pampering had kept out the weeds,
and, despite the stormy spring,

no sprigs or runners sprang from cracks
in the cobblestone drive.

No fairy rings or grubs
or spittle bugs had invaded her lawn.

I asked her what she wanted me to do,
and she said, "My husband loved this yard—

kill all of it."
She added, "Dirt will do just fine for me."

Tithing Beers

The crappie deep, I troll
my plugs, the Model A
Bombers my uncle used
in holes, off points, pre-spawn,
for fish transitioning.

One rod on either side
spread wide, one short, one long,
"curb feelers," he would say.
Back in the day, he'd wink,
"I'll tithe a Schlitz to them,"

when bites were scarce, an excuse
to drink a morning beer,
as if I didn't know
the truth, and take a slug
then dip the empty can

and fill it full with river
and let it sink. He'd tap
his pipe then pack it full.
This magic I believed in.
Something about the shine,

the wavering as it passed
by fish suspended, must
have perked their instincts right.
Always, the bite picked up.
The day he lay in bed

and said goodbye to us,
his liver gone, his gut
give up, I wanted magic
again, which never came.
He mumbled in his death

and hissed and cussed, DTs
provoking visions more
than pain or lack of food.
And when he slipped away,
my aunt said he had gone

with God. I wanted to
believe that magic, too.
I pop another beer.
I check the drags and steer
the bend. I tithe a can.

Worm on the Hook

A double omega,
Zeno's arrow suspended,
          quivers
while the universe curls its tail.

Remains

The maul my son sank deep into the heart
of a log last week remains the same as when
he missed the grain. "The wood will show you how
it wants to split," my dad would say, and I'd
look back at him—just like my son had looked
at me when I invoked with sage-like grace
those words he'd say—as if I'd stepped in shit.

No Wake Zone

Another fish camp has been razed, bait store,
crab shack. The pilings from their old piers
flaunt oyster-swollen knees at low tide.
Three stories have built up next to the landing
where I once launched my boat,
a sprawl of condos on the other side.
But for now in the no wake zone
before the mouth of the channel,
an old salt cast-nets a few mullet for the smoker.
Another man sculls a girl wearing her snorkel
through the deep swells from yachts
and out to the grass flats for scallops,
and perched on a cypress knee, Old Smokey—
a heron with one eye—recognizes my misfiring Merc.
in a channel of smooth four-strokes and inboards
and flies to the old buoy where I pitch my leftover bait.

The Silent Stones

The Watsons' pond, hard freeze—which in
the Black or Bible Belt was rare as sin,
or without God, or so our Baptist preacher ruled
we should believe. My friend and I were skipping school,

ice fishing Bama-style in store. We tossed
a brick that did not make a dent and slid
across the ice like an unanswered prayer. We flossed
some fishing line through another's cores. It did

not make a dent and broke the line and slid
into the other brick as if it were a curling stone.
"Olympics!" Scott exclaimed and grabbed a stick
shaped like a backward shepherd's crook and honed

the handle slick, removing all the bark.
I grabbed up all of Preacher Watson's bricks,
a handful at a time, and lugged them to the bank.
We slid our stones until we had our fix:

a hundred bricks or so we spread across
the ice, coal barges that had lost their tugs
or iced-in ships. Then we practiced casts with plugs
we rarely pitched for fear of losing them to snot moss.

The bricks became the spawning bass I sought.
I skated by my Zara Spook, and Scott
tied on his Hellbender and took a shot
with a long cast and snagged a stranded yacht

and pulled it in, the drag locked down, retrieve
as steady, measured as a pro until
the frayed line snapped, the lure's bill—the magic of its lilt
and shake—an iceberg jutting up.
                              The notes we deceived

our teacher with, our mamas' signatures
we looped in prideful *O*s and *P*s, didn't hide
our curling. After everyone, it seemed, had tanned our hides,
the bricks had sunk, and we had pitched enough manure

and prayed in vain for all those bricks to rise,
spring brought us back to that damned muddy sty.
The Hellbender had floated to the bank, our lie
with treble hooks fixed fast to grass like a combine's

tines. We waded out beyond the spawning beds
and dove for bricks while Preacher Watson presided
over us, chastened us beneath his breath while we wed
our giggles to a haggard twang each time we laid

a brick upon the shore. The pollen worms
from oaks were dropping everywhere. A yellow sheen
consumed our wakes when we swam back and forth,
but under water we discovered in the stones

and buried in the muck a silence we
had never felt in church or school, a silence sin
reserved for those like Judas, his silver coins
now still, like lures suspended on a frozen pond.

Sabbatical Poem [or] Time, You Mosaic of Clicking Ignitions and Broken Shoelaces

Passing over the creek swollen and rushing from three days of rain, my daughter said, "hot water," just as she has since she believed it when she was three, seeing in the creek the same roiling she saw in the spaghetti pot. I say, "yes, hot water. I wish I had a mess of crabs," and we pretend that cold as that stream is in January, it is boiling.

This morning, I am twenty-seven days from fifty. I bench-pressed weights I shouldn't be lifting alone in my basement and played "I Want You (She's So Heavy)" on repeat. I grunted and spit in the corner. I dribbled some piss in the backyard bushes.

The mailwoman seems to come earlier and earlier these days, but the clock is correct. She slides the mail in the three boxes on my cul de sac between 11:00–11:20 then parks and eats something out of Tupperware. I imagine her eating chicken divan leftovers today. I slice a hunk of manchego into thin triangles and trim the rind. I peel back the Sam's charcuterie packaging and lift the meat from the paper, then arrange it all on a green plate. I take a picture and put it on Instagram. "Ravenous," I caption it. Then I feel silly and delete it. Then I feel sad and regret deleting it, as if someone would have seen the picture and showed up at my door, sat on the floor, and eaten lunch on the ottoman with me. I play the final song from the movie *Closer* on repeat.

Out the window, a squirrel jumps from a limb my neighbor forgot to trim back this year and to the roof. She scales the pitch and crests to the other side, disappearing. She will have kits in their attic come spring. I will hear his air horn whine from the attic at nights through May. I will watch him nail flashing to the eaves where she will continue to chew through.

I pay the power bill and the cable we don't watch. I pay the cancer policy my father set up for me when I was a kid, lick the flap one full swath and then again because I taste pond water in the glue. I ruin the sticking power and have to use a length of Scotch tape. I still taste that pond water, that algae bloom and critter sex. I put the bills in the mailbox a day late. Repeat.

Collective Noun

Not a "stack" a "row" or "column"
not a "haphazard" a "jackknife" or "pileup."
Not quite a "dump" or "chum" or "scrum"
but a "baffling" of books, I decide, pulled
from the shelves and tossed
behind my desk chair the past few months.
Benedikt *Night Cries* over *Provinces of Night.*
Moore, her shadow finger tucked
behind her ear, jabs at Bishop's
Poems, the lettering the color of mustard,
"just poems," I can almost hear her intone
about the cover. Drunken lights, like a fuzzy string
of pearls, splice into a daisy chain
from *Sycamore* to *Stroke. Aliens of Affections*
sprawls across Hecht, severing the red line
that comes to a sharp point
before the cover's curled cheek. *Codes, Precepts,*
Biases, and Taboos divides *American Rendering*
and *Tasker Street* like a Cadillac taking up two spaces.
Sea Salt seeps into *The Small Blades Hurt.*
Beowulf accordions through four translations,
floundering in Heaney's Dublin captivity at the bottom.
Talking Pillow smothers all but a hint
of Larkin's starched sleeve and his shiny shoes,
The Back Country distending from the dot
of his "i" that rests on his finger
like an insignia ring with its "P"
for "poet" almost worn away.

Crab Stakes

We waded out and stuck our stakes, some quarter round
we'd snapped against our knees, into the sand at Phillip's
Inlet, the sandbar spooning off to turtle grass
and tannic water bruised like pears or "thick as Mama's
coffee," he'd always say. Then sure as shit that sappy trope

would scuttle back and raise its claws: "or Tammy's tea."
I cut the lengths of string we'd need and tied them to
the quarter round and threaded mullet heads through gills
and out the mouths and back around with the other ends.
"I'd watch TV. She'd stack those silly fucking books

she wanted me to read. I took her kid as mine.
That's life, you know. But then she shaved down there, the gym,
tattoo—hibiscus winking from her panty line
to baby-tee. I should have known it wasn't winking
at me. We had new cars. We held good jobs. Hell, we

were we." A bellied string began to straighten out,
a jerk, some slack. I inched it in. He scooped it up,
a Jimmy with one claw. Another line then trickled
out while the sun unwound its rope of orange and pink
atop the longleaf pines. "It's getting dark," I said,

"no-see-ums on the way. We better get along."
He fingered in the outstretched string, a sponger,
her apron caution orange with eggs. He lifted the string
into the air, and she swung like a pendulum
in perfect time for just a moment then let go,

or so it seemed. And though we would have had to shake
her off at any rate, according to the regs,
I tried to shun what all I knew of crabs and hoped
that he would do the same, imposing human love
on those who can't release, on those whose only drive

is appetite, how human tenderness bestows a crab,
and even if it's just an unintended slip,
a letting go when something greater is at stake.
And maybe through the parallel we draw with ourselves,

beguiling natural history and Bacon's claims,
we learn about the greater stakes and what it means
if we are we. Instead, he said, "That dumbass crab.

Tattoo and kid—she'll never find a fuck like me."
Or maybe we remain unchanged, where tenderness
is just a slip and we are all clenched claws at heart.

Pigeons at Fat Sam's

They wait for him
on power lines

in three rows
(three, six, five).

On the ridge
of Red Mountain

behind them,
Vulcan points

a spear tip
to the heaven

he was tossed from;
radio towers flanking him

blink bright enough to see
even in this 10:00 sun.

They flush
like a fistful

of pamphlets
when a plane's

shadow wets
the asphalt

below them.
Then they return

to wait for him
on power lines

in three rows
(three, six, five).

His mini-van
cuts into
the parking lot

and scuttles back
into the space
in front of the liquor store

he runs, and they flush
like a fistful
of pamphlets

and land
on his luggage racks
in two rows

(seven and seven).
He rattles some keys,
ducks inside,

and back out
with two handfuls of seed
and sows them

in front of me.
And they flush
like a fistful

of pamphlets
then land, their throats
shimmering teal

and pink while they bob,
their legs bright
arteries branching

to their capillary feet.
After they pick

the parking lot clean,
they wait for him

on power lines
in three rows

(three, six, five)
until another plane

wings by and they flush
like a fistful of pamphlets.

Two Views

1.

Who is this woman on the beach,
standing at 4 a.m., her arms
an *X* across her chest, holding
herself like someone else
anticipating loss like me?

Who is this woman on the beach,
the tide now crawling up her calves
and spitting on her lacy hem?
Does she have someone back
in bed and fast asleep like me?

2.

Who are these two unmovables,
a man, a woman split by space,
the sky now rusty light, a line
of plovers darting and pecking
and back again with each receding wave?

Who are these two unmovables,
while the sun divorces from the horizon?
An egret balances the space between,
its brittle legs a compass
measuring perfect angles and degrees.

The Golden Years

I said, "The jasmine blooms along the fence."
You set the cuckoo clocks to different times.
The bird in the hall is thirteen minutes slow.
You devil some eggs, spread out the greens to dry.

You set the cuckoo clocks to different times.
"It's Sunday; the mailman doesn't come today."
You devil some eggs, spread out the greens to dry.
You dress your childhood dolls in faded clothes.

"It's Sunday; the mailman doesn't come today,"
you said. "Tomorrow, we'll have chicken and rice."
You dress your childhood dolls in faded clothes.
You brush your hair, push back your cuticles.

You said, "Tomorrow, we'll have chicken and rice.
Your sister called again. Your hands are filthy."
You brush your hair, push back your cuticles,
take out your book, ready yourself for bed.

"Your sister called again. Your hands are filthy."
The bird in the hall is thirteen minutes slow.
"Take out your book, ready yourself for bed,"
I said. The jasmine blooms along the fence.

Memory Care

She can't remember *red,* though red is what
she wears, or elements: the wind outside,
the rain last week. She will (or won't) abide
the host this month, his dead-fish hand and cut

of cheek when he asks if she'll pray with him.
The yeses, nos have lost their way, and she
just nods at everything, her face a whim
her fancy never bears. She would have seethed

at people she now hears and doesn't hear:
"That pudding looks so good. You must be cold."
The preacher whispers in her ear a fold
of sounds, "take, eat—this is my body *here,*

given for you. This is my blood, which is
poured out for you. Now, drink." She will not part
her lips. The preacher becomes her husband: "this,
my body, this, my blood." He hits her mark.

She fingers her chest—its steady ramp—the thrum
of fluorescent lights and says, "my body, you,
my blood, the covenant we made anew,
my blood, my body. Remember us, our son?"

While Changing a Flat
on My Boat Trailer

Only in this vacancy,
the clear-cut field
on a backroad to the launch,
dawn conceding

to early morning drizzle,
would I notice
the crouched hare beside a pile
of brush, his eye

cut to the periphery,
cut back at me
then a frenzy of brown,
new vacancy.

River Politics

I spit my smack,

Jim slugs his Jack,

Rob stews his lack,

Carey prepares his rack,

herons hunker on blowdowns,

deer wait on high moon for their rounds,

and the campfire

might as well be an empire

we all

watch dissolve

(in the slough, a carp roll, a splash)

into ash.

Our Boat

—in memory of Scott Harris

Six years have passed,
and I still look starboard for you,

you who would step
without warning from the wheel

in the no wake zone,
and I would slide over like your shadow

and steer the channel markers
and crab-trap buoys

while you took a piss off the side.
Then I'd hand her back to you,

this boat I've since named The Luby,
after your daughters, Lucy and Ruby.

I'd tie on topwater plugs
or hooks and popping corks,

test our leaders for frays
with my tongue and retie new ones,

check our drags,
drags set for paper-mouth specks

on some rods, for reds on others—
we, the only two in the world

we trusted with those tasks
for each other. I'd look for nervous water

and that shimmy like pitched coins
from finger mullet or menhaden

just below the surface,
and you would mosey the boat up

to just the right distance
and kick her out of gear,

just enough space for me to toss,
for the hand line to unloop to its full length,

cinching taut around my wrist,
for the cast net's gaping mouth to fall

on the pod of baitfish.
You'd give me shit if I didn't

fill the tank with one throw:
"lazy eight—I guess we'll miss

the first-light bite" you'd say, when we both
knew that only old salts like us

who reckon this water like our children's lies
could open a perfect eight-foot O

at low tide and miss the oyster bars cragging
the bottom with a speed retrieve—

your little jabs that made us
more kin than kin.

The you'd throttle down and lift the bow
and jump up onto plane to the first

patchy bottom I would spot on the grass flats.

≈≈≈

Safe light, the sky widening orange
at the horizon this early morning,

the Gulf ahead a sheet of glass,
and I am alone but still hear

that plural possessive
you always said when talking about her—

"let's go get our boat
and sneak off to the coast."

Now that you are gone,
I've missed first light again.

I will come in for lunch and take a nap
through the hottest part of the day.

I won't catch my limit. I'll wait until
the no-see-ums have gone to wherever

they haunt before I clean the fish. I'll have
just enough to dredge and fry for dinner and three

or four crabs from the trap to boil for dessert.
Ours, yes, ours, my brother.

Preservation for the Heartbroken

The stones I placed across the creek for us
to bridge are scattered now. All who
have crossed this stretch and looked at shed and reap
of swell know me as a ghost, the shoal that tongues.

The ripples spread. You spread, my love, the darter
who took a chance and pipped. I want your gills,
the way you navigate the air and water.
The why is want; the need we breathe is now.

At fifty, the need is want and want is need.
I can't abide the dictionary's what-
we-will a moment longer, what we should
because of time, what scales we shimmer, leave behind.

CPSIA information can be obtained
at www.ICGtesting.com
Printed in the USA
LVHW020731170322
713578LV00003B/283

9 780807 176894